This budget sheet belongs to:

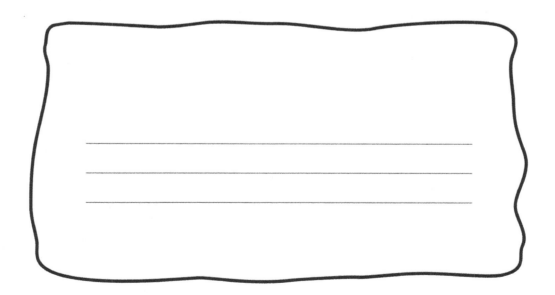

Income

Income Source	Budgeted	Amount	Remaining Income	Amount
	$	$	Total Income	$
	$	$	Total Expenses	$
	$	$	Remaining	$
Total	$	$	Total	$

Expenses

Expense	Budgeted	Amount	Expense	Budgeted	Amount
	$	$		$	$
	$	$		$	$
	$	$		$	$
	$	$		$	$
	$	$		$	$
	$	$		$	$
	$	$		$	$
	$	$		$	$
	$	$		$	$
Total	$	$	Total	$	$

Debt Repayment

Creditor	Balance	Paid
	$	$
	$	$
	$	$

Savings

Account	Goal	Amount
	$	$
	$	$

Income

Dates _____

Income Source	Budgeted	Amount	Remaining Income	Amount
	$	$	Total Income	$
	$	$	Total Expenses	$
	$	$	Remaining	$
Total	$	$	Total	$

Expenses

Expense	Budgeted	Amount	Expense	Budgeted	Amount
	$	$		$	$
	$	$		$	$
	$	$		$	$
	$	$		$	$
	$	$		$	$
	$	$		$	$
	$	$		$	$
	$	$		$	$
	$	$		$	$
Total	$	$	Total	$	$

Debt Repayment

Creditor	Balance	Paid
	$	$
	$	$
	$	$

Savings

Account	Goal	Amount
	$	$
	$	$

Income

Dates _____

Income Source	Budgeted	Amount	Remaining Income	Amount
	$	$	Total Income	$
	$	$	Total Expenses	$
	$	$	Remaining	$
Total	$	$	Total	$

Expenses

Expense	Budgeted	Amount	Expense	Budgeted	Amount
	$	$		$	$
	$	$		$	$
	$	$		$	$
	$	$		$	$
	$	$		$	$
	$	$		$	$
	$	$		$	$
	$	$		$	$
	$	$		$	$
Total	$	$	Total	$	$

Debt Repayment

Creditor	Balance	Paid
	$	$
	$	$
	$	$

Savings

Account	Goal	Amount
	$	$
	$	$

Income

Income Source	Budgeted	Amount	Remaining Income	Amount
	$	$	Total Income	$
	$	$	Total Expenses	$
	$	$	Remaining	$
Total	$	$	Total	$

Expenses

Expense	Budgeted	Amount	Expense	Budgeted	Amount
	$	$		$	$
	$	$		$	$
	$	$		$	$
	$	$		$	$
	$	$		$	$
	$	$		$	$
	$	$		$	$
	$	$		$	$
	$	$		$	$
Total	$	$	Total	$	$

Debt Repayment

Creditor	Balance	Paid
	$	$
	$	$
	$	$

Savings

Account	Goal	Amount
	$	$
	$	$

Income

Dates _____

Income Source	Budgeted	Amount	Remaining Income	Amount
	$	$	Total Income	$
	$	$	Total Expenses	$
	$	$	Remaining	$
Total	$	$	Total	$

Expenses

Expense	Budgeted	Amount	Expense	Budgeted	Amount
	$	$		$	$
	$	$		$	$
	$	$		$	$
	$	$		$	$
	$	$		$	$
	$	$		$	$
	$	$		$	$
	$	$		$	$
	$	$		$	$
Total	$	$	Total	$	$

Debt Repayment

Creditor	Balance	Paid
	$	$
	$	$
	$	$

Savings

Account	Goal	Amount
	$	$
	$	$

Income

Dates _____

Income Source	Budgeted	Amount	Remaining Income	Amount
	$	$	Total Income	$
	$	$	Total Expenses	$
	$	$	Remaining	$
Total	$	$	Total	$

Expenses

Expense	Budgeted	Amount	Expense	Budgeted	Amount
	$	$		$	$
	$	$		$	$
	$	$		$	$
	$	$		$	$
	$	$		$	$
	$	$		$	$
	$	$		$	$
	$	$		$	$
	$	$		$	$
Total	$	$	Total	$	$

Debt Repayment

Creditor	Balance	Paid
	$	$
	$	$
	$	$

Savings

Account	Goal	Amount
	$	$
	$	$

Income

Dates _____

Income Source	Budgeted	Amount	Remaining Income	Amount
	$	$	Total Income	$
	$	$	Total Expenses	$
	$	$	Remaining	$
Total	$	$	Total	$

Expenses

Expense	Budgeted	Amount	Expense	Budgeted	Amount
	$	$		$	$
	$	$		$	$
	$	$		$	$
	$	$		$	$
	$	$		$	$
	$	$		$	$
	$	$		$	$
	$	$		$	$
	$	$		$	$
Total	$	$	Total	$	$

Debt Repayment

Creditor	Balance	Paid
	$	$
	$	$
	$	$

Savings

Account	Goal	Amount
	$	$
	$	$

Income

Dates _____

Income Source	Budgeted	Amount	Remaining Income	Amount
	$	$	Total Income	$
	$	$	Total Expenses	$
	$	$	Remaining	$
Total	$	$	Total	$

Expenses

Expense	Budgeted	Amount	Expense	Budgeted	Amount
	$	$		$	$
	$	$		$	$
	$	$		$	$
	$	$		$	$
	$	$		$	$
	$	$		$	$
	$	$		$	$
	$	$		$	$
	$	$		$	$
Total	$	$	Total	$	$

Debt Repayment

Creditor	Balance	Paid
	$	$
	$	$
	$	$

Savings

Account	Goal	Amount
	$	$
	$	$

Income

Dates _____

Income Source	Budgeted	Amount	Remaining Income	Amount
	$	$	Total Income	$
	$	$	Total Expenses	$
	$	$	Remaining	$
Total	$	$	Total	$

Expenses

Expense	Budgeted	Amount	Expense	Budgeted	Amount
	$	$		$	$
	$	$		$	$
	$	$		$	$
	$	$		$	$
	$	$		$	$
	$	$		$	$
	$	$		$	$
	$	$		$	$
	$	$		$	$
Total	$	$	Total	$	$

Debt Repayment

Creditor	Balance	Paid
	$	$
	$	$
	$	$

Savings

Account	Goal	Amount
	$	$
	$	$

Income

Dates _____

Income Source	Budgeted	Amount	Remaining Income	Amount
	$	$	Total Income	$
	$	$	Total Expenses	$
	$	$	Remaining	$
Total	$	$	Total	$

Expenses

Expense	Budgeted	Amount	Expense	Budgeted	Amount
	$	$		$	$
	$	$		$	$
	$	$		$	$
	$	$		$	$
	$	$		$	$
	$	$		$	$
	$	$		$	$
	$	$		$	$
	$	$		$	$
Total	$	$	Total	$	$

Debt Repayment

Creditor	Balance	Paid
	$	$
	$	$
	$	$

Savings

Account	Goal	Amount
	$	$
	$	$

Income

Income Source	Budgeted	Amount	Remaining Income	Amount
	$	$	Total Income	$
	$	$	Total Expenses	$
	$	$	Remaining	$
Total	$	$	Total	$

Expenses

Expense	Budgeted	Amount	Expense	Budgeted	Amount
	$	$		$	$
	$	$		$	$
	$	$		$	$
	$	$		$	$
	$	$		$	$
	$	$		$	$
	$	$		$	$
	$	$		$	$
	$	$		$	$
Total	$	$	Total	$	$

Debt Repayment

Creditor	Balance	Paid
	$	$
	$	$
	$	$

Savings

Account	Goal	Amount
	$	$
	$	$

Income

Dates _____

Income Source	Budgeted	Amount	Remaining Income	Amount
	$	$	Total Income	$
	$	$	Total Expenses	$
	$	$	Remaining	$
Total	$	$	Total	$

Expenses

Expense	Budgeted	Amount	Expense	Budgeted	Amount
	$	$		$	$
	$	$		$	$
	$	$		$	$
	$	$		$	$
	$	$		$	$
	$	$		$	$
	$	$		$	$
	$	$		$	$
	$	$		$	$
Total	$	$	Total	$	$

Debt Repayment

Creditor	Balance	Paid
	$	$
	$	$
	$	$

Savings

Account	Goal	Amount
	$	$
	$	$

Income

Income Source	Budgeted	Amount	Remaining Income	Amount
	$	$	Total Income	$
	$	$	Total Expenses	$
	$	$	Remaining	$
Total	$	$	Total	$

Expenses

Expense	Budgeted	Amount	Expense	Budgeted	Amount
	$	$		$	$
	$	$		$	$
	$	$		$	$
	$	$		$	$
	$	$		$	$
	$	$		$	$
	$	$		$	$
	$	$		$	$
	$	$		$	$
Total	$	$	Total	$	$

Debt Repayment

Creditor	Balance	Paid
	$	$
	$	$
	$	$

Savings

Account	Goal	Amount
	$	$
	$	$

Income

Income Source	Budgeted	Amount	Remaining Income	Amount
	$	$	Total Income	$
	$	$	Total Expenses	$
	$	$	Remaining	$
Total	$	$	Total	$

Expenses

Expense	Budgeted	Amount	Expense	Budgeted	Amount
	$	$		$	$
	$	$		$	$
	$	$		$	$
	$	$		$	$
	$	$		$	$
	$	$		$	$
	$	$		$	$
	$	$		$	$
	$	$		$	$
Total	$	$	Total	$	$

Debt Repayment

Creditor	Balance	Paid
	$	$
	$	$
	$	$

Savings

Account	Goal	Amount
	$	$
	$	$

Income

Dates _____

Income Source	Budgeted	Amount	Remaining Income	Amount
	$	$	Total Income	$
	$	$	Total Expenses	$
	$	$	Remaining	$
Total	$	$	Total	$

Expenses

Expense	Budgeted	Amount	Expense	Budgeted	Amount
	$	$		$	$
	$	$		$	$
	$	$		$	$
	$	$		$	$
	$	$		$	$
	$	$		$	$
	$	$		$	$
	$	$		$	$
	$	$		$	$
Total	$	$	Total	$	$

Debt Repayment

Creditor	Balance	Paid
	$	$
	$	$
	$	$

Savings

Account	Goal	Amount
	$	$
	$	$

Income

Income Source	Budgeted	Amount	Remaining Income	Amount
	$	$	Total Income	$
	$	$	Total Expenses	$
	$	$	Remaining	$
Total	$	$	Total	$

Expenses

Expense	Budgeted	Amount	Expense	Budgeted	Amount
	$	$		$	$
	$	$		$	$
	$	$		$	$
	$	$		$	$
	$	$		$	$
	$	$		$	$
	$	$		$	$
	$	$		$	$
	$	$		$	$
Total	$	$	Total	$	$

Debt Repayment

Creditor	Balance	Paid
	$	$
	$	$
	$	$

Savings

Account	Goal	Amount
	$	$
	$	$

Income

Dates _____

Income Source	Budgeted	Amount	Remaining Income	Amount
	$	$	Total Income	$
	$	$	Total Expenses	$
	$	$	Remaining	$
Total	$	$	Total	$

Expenses

Expense	Budgeted	Amount	Expense	Budgeted	Amount
	$	$		$	$
	$	$		$	$
	$	$		$	$
	$	$		$	$
	$	$		$	$
	$	$		$	$
	$	$		$	$
	$	$		$	$
	$	$		$	$
Total	$	$	Total	$	$

Debt Repayment

Creditor	Balance	Paid
	$	$
	$	$
	$	$

Savings

Account	Goal	Amount
	$	$
	$	$

Income

Dates _____

Income Source	Budgeted	Amount	Remaining Income	Amount
	$	$	Total Income	$
	$	$	Total Expenses	$
	$	$	Remaining	$
Total	$	$	Total	$

Expenses

Expense	Budgeted	Amount	Expense	Budgeted	Amount
	$	$		$	$
	$	$		$	$
	$	$		$	$
	$	$		$	$
	$	$		$	$
	$	$		$	$
	$	$		$	$
	$	$		$	$
	$	$		$	$
Total	$	$	Total	$	$

Debt Repayment

Creditor	Balance	Paid
	$	$
	$	$
	$	$

Savings

Account	Goal	Amount
	$	$
	$	$

Dates _____

Income

Income Source	Budgeted	Amount	Remaining Income	Amount
	$	$	Total Income	$
	$	$	Total Expenses	$
	$	$	Remaining	$
Total	$	$	Total	$

Expenses

Expense	Budgeted	Amount	Expense	Budgeted	Amount
	$	$		$	$
	$	$		$	$
	$	$		$	$
	$	$		$	$
	$	$		$	$
	$	$		$	$
	$	$		$	$
	$	$		$	$
	$	$		$	$
Total	$	$	Total	$	$

Debt Repayment

Creditor	Balance	Paid
	$	$
	$	$
	$	$

Savings

Account	Goal	Amount
	$	$
	$	$

Income

Income Source	Budgeted	Amount	Remaining Income	Amount
	$	$	Total Income	$
	$	$	Total Expenses	$
	$	$	Remaining	$
Total	$	$	Total	$

Expenses

Expense	Budgeted	Amount	Expense	Budgeted	Amount
	$	$		$	$
	$	$		$	$
	$	$		$	$
	$	$		$	$
	$	$		$	$
	$	$		$	$
	$	$		$	$
	$	$		$	$
	$	$		$	$
Total	$	$	Total	$	$

Debt Repayment

Creditor	Balance	Paid
	$	$
	$	$
	$	$

Savings

Account	Goal	Amount
	$	$
	$	$

Dates _____

Income

Income Source	Budgeted	Amount	Remaining Income	Amount
	$	$	Total Income	$
	$	$	Total Expenses	$
	$	$	Remaining	$
Total	$	$	Total	$

Expenses

Expense	Budgeted	Amount	Expense	Budgeted	Amount
	$	$		$	$
	$	$		$	$
	$	$		$	$
	$	$		$	$
	$	$		$	$
	$	$		$	$
	$	$		$	$
	$	$		$	$
	$	$		$	$
Total	$	$	Total	$	$

Debt Repayment

Creditor	Balance	Paid
	$	$
	$	$
	$	$

Savings

Account	Goal	Amount
	$	$
	$	$

Income

Income Source	Budgeted	Amount	Remaining Income	Amount
	$	$	Total Income	$
	$	$	Total Expenses	$
	$	$	Remaining	$
Total	$	$	Total	$

Expenses

Expense	Budgeted	Amount	Expense	Budgeted	Amount
	$	$		$	$
	$	$		$	$
	$	$		$	$
	$	$		$	$
	$	$		$	$
	$	$		$	$
	$	$		$	$
	$	$		$	$
	$	$		$	$
Total	$	$	Total	$	$

Debt Repayment

Creditor	Balance	Paid
	$	$
	$	$
	$	$

Savings

Account	Goal	Amount
	$	$
	$	$

Income

Income Source	Budgeted	Amount	Remaining Income	Amount
	$	$	Total Income	$
	$	$	Total Expenses	$
	$	$	Remaining	$
Total	$	$	Total	$

Expenses

Expense	Budgeted	Amount	Expense	Budgeted	Amount
	$	$		$	$
	$	$		$	$
	$	$		$	$
	$	$		$	$
	$	$		$	$
	$	$		$	$
	$	$		$	$
	$	$		$	$
	$	$		$	$
Total	$	$	Total	$	$

Debt Repayment

Creditor	Balance	Paid
	$	$
	$	$
	$	$

Savings

Account	Goal	Amount
	$	$
	$	$

Income

Income Source	Budgeted	Amount	Remaining Income	Amount
	$	$	Total Income	$
	$	$	Total Expenses	$
	$	$	Remaining	$
Total	$	$	Total	$

Expenses

Expense	Budgeted	Amount	Expense	Budgeted	Amount
	$	$		$	$
	$	$		$	$
	$	$		$	$
	$	$		$	$
	$	$		$	$
	$	$		$	$
	$	$		$	$
	$	$		$	$
	$	$		$	$
Total	$	$	Total	$	$

Debt Repayment

Creditor	Balance	Paid
	$	$
	$	$
	$	$

Savings

Account	Goal	Amount
	$	$
	$	$

Income

Dates _____

Income Source	Budgeted	Amount	Remaining Income	Amount
	$	$	Total Income	$
	$	$	Total Expenses	$
	$	$	Remaining	$
Total	$	$	Total	$

Expenses

Expense	Budgeted	Amount	Expense	Budgeted	Amount
	$	$		$	$
	$	$		$	$
	$	$		$	$
	$	$		$	$
	$	$		$	$
	$	$		$	$
	$	$		$	$
	$	$		$	$
	$	$		$	$
Total	$	$	Total	$	$

Debt Repayment

Creditor	Balance	Paid
	$	$
	$	$
	$	$

Savings

Account	Goal	Amount
	$	$
	$	$

Income

Income Source	Budgeted	Amount	Remaining Income	Amount
	$	$	Total Income	$
	$	$	Total Expenses	$
	$	$	Remaining	$
Total	$	$	Total	$

Expenses

Expense	Budgeted	Amount	Expense	Budgeted	Amount
	$	$		$	$
	$	$		$	$
	$	$		$	$
	$	$		$	$
	$	$		$	$
	$	$		$	$
	$	$		$	$
	$	$		$	$
	$	$		$	$
Total	$	$	Total	$	$

Debt Repayment

Creditor	Balance	Paid
	$	$
	$	$
	$	$

Savings

Account	Goal	Amount
	$	$
	$	$

Income

Income Source	Budgeted	Amount	Remaining Income	Amount
	$	$	Total Income	$
	$	$	Total Expenses	$
	$	$	Remaining	$
Total	$	$	Total	$

Expenses

Expense	Budgeted	Amount	Expense	Budgeted	Amount
	$	$		$	$
	$	$		$	$
	$	$		$	$
	$	$		$	$
	$	$		$	$
	$	$		$	$
	$	$		$	$
	$	$		$	$
	$	$		$	$
Total	$	$	Total	$	$

Debt Repayment

Creditor	Balance	Paid
	$	$
	$	$
	$	$

Savings

Account	Goal	Amount
	$	$
	$	$
	$	$

Income

Income Source	Budgeted	Amount	Remaining Income	Amount
	$	$	Total Income	$
	$	$	Total Expenses	$
	$	$	Remaining	$
Total	$	$	Total	$

Expenses

Expense	Budgeted	Amount	Expense	Budgeted	Amount
	$	$		$	$
	$	$		$	$
	$	$		$	$
	$	$		$	$
	$	$		$	$
	$	$		$	$
	$	$		$	$
	$	$		$	$
	$	$		$	$
Total	$	$	Total	$	$

Debt Repayment

Creditor	Balance	Paid
	$	$
	$	$
	$	$

Savings

Account	Goal	Amount
	$	$
	$	$

Income

Income Source	Budgeted	Amount	Remaining Income	Amount
	$	$	Total Income	$
	$	$	Total Expenses	$
	$	$	Remaining	$
Total	$	$	Total	$

Expenses

Expense	Budgeted	Amount	Expense	Budgeted	Amount
	$	$		$	$
	$	$		$	$
	$	$		$	$
	$	$		$	$
	$	$		$	$
	$	$		$	$
	$	$		$	$
	$	$		$	$
	$	$		$	$
Total	$	$	Total	$	$

Debt Repayment

Creditor	Balance	Paid
	$	$
	$	$
	$	$

Savings

Account	Goal	Amount
	$	$
	$	$

Income

Dates _____

Income Source	Budgeted	Amount	Remaining Income	Amount
	$	$	Total Income	$
	$	$	Total Expenses	$
	$	$	Remaining	$
Total	$	$	Total	$

Expenses

Expense	Budgeted	Amount	Expense	Budgeted	Amount
	$	$		$	$
	$	$		$	$
	$	$		$	$
	$	$		$	$
	$	$		$	$
	$	$		$	$
	$	$		$	$
	$	$		$	$
	$	$		$	$
Total	$	$	Total	$	$

Debt Repayment

Creditor	Balance	Paid
	$	$
	$	$
	$	$

Savings

Account	Goal	Amount
	$	$
	$	$

Income

Income Source	Budgeted	Amount	Remaining Income	Amount
	$	$	Total Income	$
	$	$	Total Expenses	$
	$	$	Remaining	$
Total	$	$	Total	$

Expenses

Expense	Budgeted	Amount	Expense	Budgeted	Amount
	$	$		$	$
	$	$		$	$
	$	$		$	$
	$	$		$	$
	$	$		$	$
	$	$		$	$
	$	$		$	$
	$	$		$	$
	$	$		$	$
Total	$	$	Total	$	$

Debt Repayment

Creditor	Balance	Paid
	$	$
	$	$
	$	$

Savings

Account	Goal	Amount
	$	$
	$	$

Income

Dates _____

Income Source	Budgeted	Amount	Remaining Income	Amount
	$	$	Total Income	$
	$	$	Total Expenses	$
	$	$	Remaining	$
Total	$	$	Total	$

Expenses

Expense	Budgeted	Amount	Expense	Budgeted	Amount
	$	$		$	$
	$	$		$	$
	$	$		$	$
	$	$		$	$
	$	$		$	$
	$	$		$	$
	$	$		$	$
	$	$		$	$
	$	$		$	$
Total	$	$	Total	$	$

Debt Repayment

Creditor	Balance	Paid
	$	$
	$	$
	$	$

Savings

Account	Goal	Amount
	$	$
	$	$

Income

Dates _____

Income Source	Budgeted	Amount	Remaining Income	Amount
	$	$	Total Income	$
	$	$	Total Expenses	$
	$	$	Remaining	$
Total	$	$	Total	$

Expenses

Expense	Budgeted	Amount	Expense	Budgeted	Amount
	$	$		$	$
	$	$		$	$
	$	$		$	$
	$	$		$	$
	$	$		$	$
	$	$		$	$
	$	$		$	$
	$	$		$	$
	$	$		$	$
Total	$	$	Total	$	$

Debt Repayment

Creditor	Balance	Paid
	$	$
	$	$
	$	$

Savings

Account	Goal	Amount
	$	$
	$	$

Income

Dates _____

Income Source	Budgeted	Amount	Remaining Income	Amount
	$	$	Total Income	$
	$	$	Total Expenses	$
	$	$	Remaining	$
Total	$	$	Total	$

Expenses

Expense	Budgeted	Amount	Expense	Budgeted	Amount
	$	$		$	$
	$	$		$	$
	$	$		$	$
	$	$		$	$
	$	$		$	$
	$	$		$	$
	$	$		$	$
	$	$		$	$
	$	$		$	$
Total	$	$	Total	$	$

Debt Repayment

Creditor	Balance	Paid
	$	$
	$	$
	$	$

Savings

Account	Goal	Amount
	$	$
	$	$

Income

Income Source	Budgeted	Amount	Remaining Income	Amount
	$	$	Total Income	$
	$	$	Total Expenses	$
	$	$	Remaining	$
Total	$	$	Total	$

Expenses

Expense	Budgeted	Amount	Expense	Budgeted	Amount
	$	$		$	$
	$	$		$	$
	$	$		$	$
	$	$		$	$
	$	$		$	$
	$	$		$	$
	$	$		$	$
	$	$		$	$
	$	$		$	$
Total	$	$	Total	$	$

Debt Repayment

Creditor	Balance	Paid
	$	$
	$	$
	$	$

Savings

Account	Goal	Amount
	$	$
	$	$

Income

Income Source	Budgeted	Amount	Remaining Income	Amount
	$	$	Total Income	$
	$	$	Total Expenses	$
	$	$	Remaining	$
Total	$	$	Total	$

Expenses

Expense	Budgeted	Amount	Expense	Budgeted	Amount
	$	$		$	$
	$	$		$	$
	$	$		$	$
	$	$		$	$
	$	$		$	$
	$	$		$	$
	$	$		$	$
	$	$		$	$
	$	$		$	$
Total	$	$	Total	$	$

Debt Repayment

Creditor	Balance	Paid
	$	$
	$	$
	$	$

Savings

Account	Goal	Amount
	$	$
	$	$

Dates _____

Income

Income Source	Budgeted	Amount	Remaining Income	Amount
	$	$	Total Income	$
	$	$	Total Expenses	$
	$	$	Remaining	$
Total	$	$	Total	$

Expenses

Expense	Budgeted	Amount	Expense	Budgeted	Amount
	$	$		$	$
	$	$		$	$
	$	$		$	$
	$	$		$	$
	$	$		$	$
	$	$		$	$
	$	$		$	$
	$	$		$	$
	$	$		$	$
Total	$	$	Total	$	$

Debt Repayment

Creditor	Balance	Paid
	$	$
	$	$
	$	$

Savings

Account	Goal	Amount
	$	$
	$	$

Income

Income Source	Budgeted	Amount	Remaining Income	Amount
	$	$	Total Income	$
	$	$	Total Expenses	$
	$	$	Remaining	$
Total	$	$	Total	$

Expenses

Expense	Budgeted	Amount	Expense	Budgeted	Amount
	$	$		$	$
	$	$		$	$
	$	$		$	$
	$	$		$	$
	$	$		$	$
	$	$		$	$
	$	$		$	$
	$	$		$	$
	$	$		$	$
Total	$	$	Total	$	$

Debt Repayment

Creditor	Balance	Paid
	$	$
	$	$
	$	$

Savings

Account	Goal	Amount
	$	$
	$	$

Income

Income Source	Budgeted	Amount	Remaining Income	Amount
	$	$	Total Income	$
	$	$	Total Expenses	$
	$	$	Remaining	$
Total	$	$	Total	$

Expenses

Expense	Budgeted	Amount	Expense	Budgeted	Amount
	$	$		$	$
	$	$		$	$
	$	$		$	$
	$	$		$	$
	$	$		$	$
	$	$		$	$
	$	$		$	$
	$	$		$	$
	$	$		$	$
Total	$	$	Total	$	$

Debt Repayment

Creditor	Balance	Paid
	$	$
	$	$
	$	$

Savings

Account	Goal	Amount
	$	$
	$	$

Income

Income Source	Budgeted	Amount	Remaining Income	Amount
	$	$	Total Income	$
	$	$	Total Expenses	$
	$	$	Remaining	$
Total	$	$	Total	$

Expenses

Expense	Budgeted	Amount	Expense	Budgeted	Amount
	$	$		$	$
	$	$		$	$
	$	$		$	$
	$	$		$	$
	$	$		$	$
	$	$		$	$
	$	$		$	$
	$	$		$	$
	$	$		$	$
Total	$	$	Total	$	$

Debt Repayment

Creditor	Balance	Paid
	$	$
	$	$
	$	$

Savings

Account	Goal	Amount
	$	$
	$	$

Income

Income Source	Budgeted	Amount	Remaining Income	Amount
	$	$	Total Income	$
	$	$	Total Expenses	$
	$	$	Remaining	$
Total	$	$	Total	$

Expenses

Expense	Budgeted	Amount	Expense	Budgeted	Amount
	$	$		$	$
	$	$		$	$
	$	$		$	$
	$	$		$	$
	$	$		$	$
	$	$		$	$
	$	$		$	$
	$	$		$	$
	$	$		$	$
Total	$	$	Total	$	$

Debt Repayment

Creditor	Balance	Paid
	$	$
	$	$
	$	$

Savings

Account	Goal	Amount
	$	$
	$	$

Income

Dates _____

Income Source	Budgeted	Amount	Remaining Income	Amount
	$	$	Total Income	$
	$	$	Total Expenses	$
	$	$	Remaining	$
Total	$	$	Total	$

Expenses

Expense	Budgeted	Amount	Expense	Budgeted	Amount
	$	$		$	$
	$	$		$	$
	$	$		$	$
	$	$		$	$
	$	$		$	$
	$	$		$	$
	$	$		$	$
	$	$		$	$
	$	$		$	$
Total	$	$	Total	$	$

Debt Repayment

Creditor	Balance	Paid
	$	$
	$	$
	$	$

Savings

Account	Goal	Amount
	$	$
	$	$

Dates _____

Income

Income Source	Budgeted	Amount	Remaining Income	Amount
	$	$	Total Income	$
	$	$	Total Expenses	$
	$	$	Remaining	$
Total	$	$	Total	$

Expenses

Expense	Budgeted	Amount	Expense	Budgeted	Amount
	$	$		$	$
	$	$		$	$
	$	$		$	$
	$	$		$	$
	$	$		$	$
	$	$		$	$
	$	$		$	$
	$	$		$	$
	$	$		$	$
Total	$	$	Total	$	$

Debt Repayment

Creditor	Balance	Paid
	$	$
	$	$
	$	$

Savings

Account	Goal	Amount
	$	$
	$	$

Income

Income Source	Budgeted	Amount	Remaining Income	Amount
	$	$	Total Income	$
	$	$	Total Expenses	$
	$	$	Remaining	$
Total	$	$	Total	$

Expenses

Expense	Budgeted	Amount	Expense	Budgeted	Amount
	$	$		$	$
	$	$		$	$
	$	$		$	$
	$	$		$	$
	$	$		$	$
	$	$		$	$
	$	$		$	$
	$	$		$	$
	$	$		$	$
Total	$	$	Total	$	$

Debt Repayment

Creditor	Balance	Paid
	$	$
	$	$
	$	$

Savings

Account	Goal	Amount
	$	$
	$	$

Income

Income Source	Budgeted	Amount	Remaining Income	Amount
	$	$	Total Income	$
	$	$	Total Expenses	$
	$	$	Remaining	$
Total	$	$	Total	$

Expenses

Expense	Budgeted	Amount	Expense	Budgeted	Amount
	$	$		$	$
	$	$		$	$
	$	$		$	$
	$	$		$	$
	$	$		$	$
	$	$		$	$
	$	$		$	$
	$	$		$	$
	$	$		$	$
Total	$	$	Total	$	$

Debt Repayment

Creditor	Balance	Paid
	$	$
	$	$
	$	$

Savings

Account	Goal	Amount
	$	$
	$	$

Dates _____

Income

Income Source	Budgeted	Amount	Remaining Income	Amount
	$	$	Total Income	$
	$	$	Total Expenses	$
	$	$	Remaining	$
Total	$	$	Total	$

Expenses

Expense	Budgeted	Amount	Expense	Budgeted	Amount
	$	$		$	$
	$	$		$	$
	$	$		$	$
	$	$		$	$
	$	$		$	$
	$	$		$	$
	$	$		$	$
	$	$		$	$
	$	$		$	$
Total	$	$	Total	$	$

Debt Repayment

Creditor	Balance	Paid
	$	$
	$	$
	$	$

Savings

Account	Goal	Amount
	$	$
	$	$

Income

Dates _____

Income Source	Budgeted	Amount	Remaining Income	Amount
	$	$	Total Income	$
	$	$	Total Expenses	$
	$	$	Remaining	$
Total	$	$	Total	$

Expenses

Expense	Budgeted	Amount	Expense	Budgeted	Amount
	$	$		$	$
	$	$		$	$
	$	$		$	$
	$	$		$	$
	$	$		$	$
	$	$		$	$
	$	$		$	$
	$	$		$	$
	$	$		$	$
Total	$	$	Total	$	$

Debt Repayment

Creditor	Balance	Paid
	$	$
	$	$
	$	$

Savings

Account	Goal	Amount
	$	$
	$	$

Income

Income Source	Budgeted	Amount	Remaining Income	Amount
	$	$	Total Income	$
	$	$	Total Expenses	$
	$	$	Remaining	$
Total	$	$	Total	$

Expenses

Expense	Budgeted	Amount	Expense	Budgeted	Amount
	$	$		$	$
	$	$		$	$
	$	$		$	$
	$	$		$	$
	$	$		$	$
	$	$		$	$
	$	$		$	$
	$	$		$	$
	$	$		$	$
Total	$	$	Total	$	$

Debt Repayment

Creditor	Balance	Paid
	$	$
	$	$
	$	$

Savings

Account	Goal	Amount
	$	$
	$	$

Made in the USA
Las Vegas, NV
12 May 2022

48799291R00031